8899. Spalding's Black End Wagon Tongue Bat, genuine League quality, made of finest straight grained ash. Handle is roughened by a patent process, for a better grip. Retails at twice our price. Each...$0.60

8900. Spalding's Black End "Axletree" Bat, made finest, straight grained ash, improved models. The best bat ever sold at anything like the price, and one at will please amateur and professional alike. ach...$0.40

8906. Spalding's Black End "Antique" Finish Bat, ade of extra quality ash. Very strong and well ade. Each...$0.20

8907. Spalding's Black End Willow Bat, very highly ished with shellac and polished. The best and rongest light bat ever sold. Each.............$0.35
8908. Spalding's Black End Boys' Axletree Bat, ry fine, extra quality ash, lengths 30 and 32 inches. special grade that will give best satisfaction. .ch...$0.20
8909. Spalding's Black End Youth's Maple Bat, ined and polished, and decorated with gilt stripes. tra value and worth double the money. Each..$0.10

8910. Spalding's Black End, Boys' Maple Bat, plain ish with gilt stripes, a dandy bat for a few pennies. .ch...............$0.04 Per dozen.............$0.45

BASE BALL MITTS.

r stock includes all kinds, Catchers, Basemen's, Iners' Mitts, as well as Infielders' Gloves, all of the best that can be made. Special inducements to s purchasing $20.00 or more at one time. Our terms ll orders of $5.00 or more are very liberal. C. O. D., ect to examination on receipt of one-fourth of order.

SPALDING'S CATCHERS' MITTS.

l of our Mitts are furnished for either the right or hand. The Left Hand Mitt always sent unless rwise ordered. **No Throwing Glove** furnished any of our Mitts this season.

No. 8912,

No. 8912. Basemen's Mitt. This Mitt bearing the trade mark of our highest quality goods, is sufficient guarantee that it is the most perfect glove in all its details that our past experience enables us to produce. The leather is of the finest quality adapted for that purpose, the padding and workmanship of the very best, and the additional feature of lace back make it—as we intend it shall be—the "PERFECTION" of Catchers' Mitts. Made in rights and lefts. Regular price.....$7.50 Our price, each.................$5.50

No. 8913. The "Morrill" Mitt is after the design of the well-known ball player, John Morrill, and has become very popular. It is made throughout of finest quality drab buckskin, is very heavily padded

quality asbestos buck, perspiration proof and extremely tough and durable. It has our patent lace back, reinforced at thumb and well made and padded. Made in rights and lefts. Each.................................$1.65

No. 8918.

No. 8918. The Spalding Practice Mitt. The face and finger-piece of our Practice Mitt are made of light brown tanned suede leather, the edge strip and back of ecru tanned suede. It has our patent lace back, reinforced at thumb and substantially padded. Made in rights and lefts. Each 75c

SPALDING'S BOYS' CATCH-ERS' MITTS.

No. 8920.

No. 8919. Spalding's "Decker Patent" Boys' League Mitt; face, edge strip and finger-piece made of velvet tanned deerskin, the back of fine hogskin, very soft and perspiration proof. The heavy piece of sole leather on back affords extra protection to hand and fingers. It has the patent lace back and is extra well padded. Made in rights and lefts. Each.......$1.80

No. 8920. Spalding's Boys' Mitt; face and finger-piece of mitt made of dark tanned leather, the back and edge strip of light tanned asbestos buck. It has our patent lace back, well padded and finished and reinforced at thumb. Made in rights and lefts, and little larger in size than our regular Boys' Mitts. Each $1.25

No. 8921.

No. 8921. Spalding's Boys' Mitts; front and finger-piece of this mitt are made of light brown tanned suede leather, the back and edge strip ecru tanned. It is extremely well padded and nicely finished throughout, and has our patent lace back. Made in rights and lefts. Each.........................39c

No. 8922.

No. 8922. Spalding's Boys' Mitt; front and back made of ecru tanned leather, the edge strip of lighter tanned leather. Well made throughout, heavily padded and superior to any boys' mitt ever offered at the price. Each....................20c

SPALDING'S BASEMEN'S MITT.

No. 8923.

No. 8923. Basemen's Mitt, made of fine selected and specially tanned calfskin, extremely well made throughout and padded to meet the special requirements of a baseman's mitt. It adapts itself nicely to the conformation of the hand without undue straining, and the addition of our patent lace back and "Highest Quality" trade mark is a sufficient guarantee of its quality and merits. Made in rights and lefts. Each.......$3.60

SPALDING'S BASEMEN'S AND INFIELDERS' MITTS.

No. 8924. Mitt, made of the very best and softest light tanned buckskin; the thumb and at wrist are extra well padded with the highest quality felt, making it a very safe and easy fit-

glove is perfect in all it
Made in rights and lefts.
Each...................

No. 8928.

INFIELDERS' GLO

No. 8929. Spalding's Infielder made of suede leather, li padded with felt and careful gether. Made in rights and le Each...................
No. 8930. Spalding's Men's Glove, all leather; a substanti a popular price. Each.......

BOYS' INFIELDER GLOVES.

No. 8929.

No. 8931. Spalding's Boys' Glove, quality and style as ou in boys' sizes. Each.........

PITCHER'S T PLATES.

Worn on toe of shoe, and left or right foot. A valua ant in pitching.
No. 8932. Aluminum toe pla
....
No. 8933. Brass toe plate.

SPALDING'S MASKS.

Black Enameled Sun
No. 8935. Mask—Patented
Spalding's League. This is not
"Highest Quality" ma
but has also patent s
which is formed by a
molded leather securely
to top, forming a perfec
the eye without obstru
view or materially incre
weight of the mask.
best soft annealed steel
No. 8935. tra heavy and black e
thus further preventing the reflection of li
mask throughout is constructed of the very
terial and has been highly endorsed by th
catchers. Each..........................

SPALDING'S BLACK ENAME MASKS.

No. 8936.

No. 8936.

No. 8936. Patent Neck Protec has an extension at bottom solute protection to the nec interfering in the least movements of the head. T of best annealed steel, is ex and covered with black e prevent the reflection of lig padding is filled with goat faced with finest imported which, being impervious to tion, always remains soft a ant to the face. Each....

No. 8938.

No. 8937. Special League Ma of extra heavy and best nealed steel wire, black e the padding filled with goat covered with finest impor skin. Each..............
No. 8938. Regulation Leagu made of heavy soft annea wire, black enameled, the well stuffed and faced with tanned horsehide. Warran class and reliable in every p Each ....

REGULATION LEAGUE MASK

No. 8939. This mask is of same

LIFE IN AMERICA 100 YEARS AGO

Sports and Recreation

Sports and Recreation

David Ritchie

Chelsea House Publishers

New York   Philadelphia

CHELSEA HOUSE PUBLISHERS

Editorial Director: Richard Rennert
Executive Managing Editor: Karyn Gullen Browne
Copy Chief: Robin James
Picture Editor: Adrian G. Allen
Creative Director: Robert Mitchell
Art Director: Joan Ferrigno
Production Manager: Sallye Scott

LIFE IN AMERICA 100 YEARS AGO
Senior Editor: Jake Goldberg

Staff for Sports and Recreation
Editorial Assistant: Erin McKenna
Designer: Lydia Rivera
Picture Researcher: Sandy Jones
Cover Illustrator: Steve Cieslawski

3 5 7 9 8 6 4 2
Library of Congress Cataloging-in-Publication Data

Ritchie, David
    Sports and recreation David Ritchie.
    p. cm.—(Life in America 100 years ago)
    Includes bibliographical references and index.
    ISBN 0-7910-2848-8
    1. Recreation—United States—History—19th century. 2. Amusements—United
States—History—19th century. 3. Sports—United States—History—19th century. I. Title.
II. Series.
    GV53.R58 1996
    790'.0973'09034—dc20

95-4605
CIP
AC

CONTENTS

LIFE IN AMERICA 100 YEARS AGO

Communication

Education

Frontier Life

Government and Politics

Health and Medicine

Industry and Business

Law and Order

Manners and Customs

Sports and Recreation

Transportation

Urban Life

Sports and Recreation

Pastimes of a Past Century

THE MODERN AGE IS THE AGE OF SPORTS. AT LEAST, ONE would think so after seeing how they dominate our lives. Every hour of every day, television, radio, newspapers, and magazines provide sports coverage. For many people the Super Bowl or the World Series is the high point of the year. The sports section is the first part of the daily newspaper that many people read.

Sports stadiums dominate cities. Communities live for their local teams. When a team leaves one city for another, the loss is treated like that of a major industry. Sports matches can even polarize a community to the point of violence. Success in sports is often equated with success in life; prominent coaches and players become heroes, and their lives are the stuff of household conversation and made-for-TV movies.

This obsession with sports would have astonished people more than 100 years ago. In the mid–19th century the sports industry as we know it did not exist, and neither did many sports that we now watch and play. Baseball had just appeared, and basketball had not

Horse racing has been popular in the United States since around 1800.

been invented yet. The term "pro athlete" was meaningless, and the notion that an athlete might receive $2 million or more for playing at a professional sports event would have been inconceivable in the early 1800s. There were times in the 19th century when the whole federal treasury contained only about $100,000. When the first professional football player finally came along in 1892, he was paid the grand sum of $500 for a game. Of course, at the time that was a considerable sum of money, but nothing like what professional athletes are paid today.

If you mentioned night games to people living in the mid-1800s, you would have received puzzled stares in response. Play games

10

outdoors at night? How would you see? The lightbulb had not yet been invented. The nights were dark, and people either worked or read by candles or oil lamps or went to bed early. More people were farmers in those days, and nightlife was restricted by the need to get a good night's sleep, rise early, and begin the day's chores.

On the other hand, today's sports enthusiasts might have trouble guessing what their ancestors were talking about when they mentioned games like skittles and rounders, or walking races. Who would want to watch people walking?

This women's footrace at Lake Huntington, New York, reflects the 19th-century interest in sports for improving women's health.

Boxing, or pugilism, became disreputable in the mid-1800s, but in time reforms improved its reputation.

Beyond specific games, however, there is an even more profound difference between sports today and the amusements of the 1800s. The whole concept of sports itself has changed. Although the difference appears at first to be merely one of more money and larger audiences, it is actually much more complex than that. The transition from 19th-century games and recreation to 20th-century sports involved a great web of interconnected changes in social institutions, industry, and technology.

Sports and recreation in the early 1800s were not entirely different from what we know today. Horse racing in the early 1800s, for example, was much as it is now. Some races drew vast numbers of

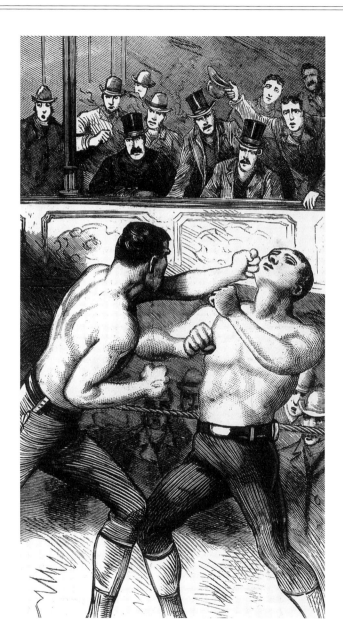

Boxing was as popular in the 1800s as it is now. Note the absence of gloves on these 19th-century boxers.

spectators. A horse race in 1823 at Union Park, New York, drew a crowd estimated at more than 60,000 people.

Bowling was familiar to Americans in the early 1800s. Washington Irving mentions it in his famous tale of Rip Van Winkle, published in

Golf was played in the United States long before this scene was drawn in 1887. Scottish officers in British forces played golf in America in colonial days.

1819. Known as bowling at pins, ninepins, or skittles, the game involved rolling a ball toward a cluster of nine pins and knocking them down. Irving compared the sound of the ball hitting the pins to thunder. Ninepin bowling was notorious for the gambling activities that surrounded it, and many games were rigged. Some people who refused to cooperate with the fix were beaten up by hired thugs. Corruption in sports is not unique to our own times.

Eventually bowling became so corrupt that several states banned the game of ninepins. The game went on, however, because of a loophole; though ninepin bowling was prohibited, the law said nothing about 10-pin bowling. So a 10th pin was added, and the game became lawful again.

Gambling appears to have been almost a national mania among 19th-century Americans. A card game called faro was especially popular. The image of the shady riverboat gambler of western lore has much basis in fact. The culture of gambling in 19th-century America was interwoven with sports and recreation, just as it is now.

Boxing was a familiar sport in 19th-century America. In the early 1800s, boxing provided an interesting study in class divisions. In cities, boxing was mainly an upper-class sport practiced by wealthy young men. In rural areas, on the other hand, slaves might compete to see who was the best boxer. A slave could win his freedom in the boxing ring. One slave who did so was the great boxer Tom Molyneux, who went on to fight in England. By the mid-1800s boxing had become a sport for the middle and lower classes. It became so disreputable after the Civil War that boxing was banned in many communities. Adopting the Marquis of Queensbury rules restored boxing to respectability in the late 1800s, and some boxers, including the famous John L. Sullivan, became early heroes of the sport.

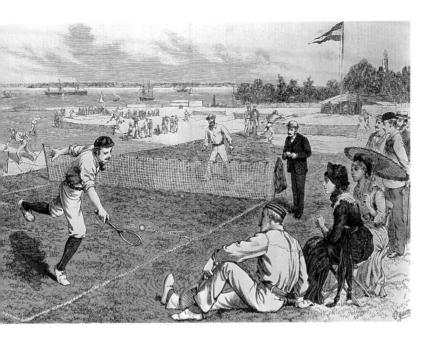

Tennis was introduced to the United States from Britain by way of Bermuda, where an American visitor saw the game being played and decided to bring it to the United States. This engraving shows the first national lawn tennis tournament, on Staten Island, New York, in 1880.

Golf was another popular sport of 19th-century America. It had been brought to the United States by Scottish officers in the British army stationed in the colonies. The first American club for golfers was established soon after a Scot named John Reid installed a six-hole course near his home in Yonkers, New York, in 1888. The modern 18-hole course appeared later.

Archery was a popular outdoor sport of the 1800s, attracting both men and women, and croquet enjoyed great success between the middle and late 1800s but declined dramatically by 1900. Angling, or fishing, was also popular in the 19th century, as were roller-skating and ice-skating.

Nineteenth-century Americans were fond of rowing. They even introduced a successful innovation: the sliding seat. Early models

Women's tennis is more than a century old. Female U.S. international tennis players assemble for a photograph in 1895.

With roller skates, one did not have to wait for winter to go skating. This illustration shows an indoor skating rink in Vienna in 1876. Note the orchestra in the gallery.

slipped back and forth on runners or grooves. Later, the seat was mounted on wheels. Rowing became the first intercollegiate sport in the United States. The earliest rowing match between American colleges took place in 1852, when Harvard rowed against Yale.

Foxhunting was beloved by the upper classes in the southern states. The planter class imitated the habits and pleasures of the English aristocrats. The hunters wore elegant riding outfits and pursued the fox across the fields on horseback. A foxhunt was a lively pastime, although it ended brutally for the fox.

Other 19th-century sports were quite cruel to animals by modern standards. For example, fights were arranged between bears and bulls. The Wall Street expressions "bear" and "bull," referring to changes in the stock market, reportedly originated with these contests. Cockfighting, in which roosters were pitted against each other, was another popular sport that eventually fell into disfavor because of reactions against animal cruelty.

A curious 19th-century sport was the walking race. Popular around 1850, it involved purposeful walking over a designated course. Some races covered distances of 20 miles or more. Large crowds would gather to watch a walking race.

Track-and-field events became popular in the United States around 1850. The Caledonian Clubs in Boston and New York organized track-and-field events, including sack races and the standing high jump. In 1868 the New York Athletic Club, which held indoor track-and-field games, was founded. Many other athletic clubs soon arose in cities all over the United States.

Perhaps the greatest day for sports and outdoor recreation in 19th-century America was the Fourth of July, Independence Day. Virtually the whole population of a town would turn out for festivities that ended at night with a fireworks display. So beloved were Independence Day revels that when the mining town of Rough and Ready, California, chose to secede from the United States in 1850 in a protest over onerous state and federal taxes, the townsfolk reconsidered and rejoined the United States when they stopped to think that secession would mean an end to Fourth of July celebrations.

Cities and rural areas differed in the sports they preferred. Sports took on a special character along the frontier. Wrestling was popular; President Abraham Lincoln was a wrestler in his youth. Hunting on the frontier was not a sport in the way that foxhunts were. The upper crust pursued foxes for fun, but frontier settlers hunted for food. Practicing marksmanship skills for hunting became the basis for a new frontier sport—the shooting match. A shooting match might be held at the same time as other recreations such as footraces or quoits, a game similar to pitching horseshoes. Other frontier entertainments included the rodeo, where cowboys would demonstrate their skill at roping cattle.

Since frontier folk faced much heavy and tedious labor, they tried to lighten their burdens through bees, friendly challenges that turned work into sport. Settlers would get together to see who was best at chopping wood or some other activity. In this way the work got done and neighbors had a chance to socialize. Dances and other social functions served much the same purpose as bees.

Gymnastics were part of the curriculum at the Turnverein, a combined school and social center founded by immigrant Germans in the mid-1800s. The Turnverein curriculum was similar to physical education programs of 20th-century schools. Similar programs became available through the Young Men's Christian Association (YMCA) and the Young Women's Christian Association (YWCA).

Music and the theater were also popular sources of entertainment. Even in the tiny mining community of Volcano, California, a local theatrical group performed in the 1850s. Performances did not always go as planned. In Pitkin, Colorado, a special effects man once substituted fireworks for electrical lighting in a theater. They produced clouds of smoke that made the audience flee.

Fencing was a popular sport in the 1800s and early 1900s. Here a female competitor poses for a picture.

New technology affected sports dramatically during the 19th century. An example of this was the development of the bicycle. From early, rough-riding models, the bicycle had been transformed by the 1870s into the famous highwheeler, on which cyclists sat atop an enormous front wheel almost as tall as a grown man. The rear wheel was comparatively tiny. Though costly and dangerous (one could get injured falling from the high seat), these machines were marketed successfully. All cyclists were men, since a woman in a dress could not use the pedals. The introduction of the safety bicycle in the late 1880s made cycling safer and extended its appeal to women.

Tennis was imported to the United States from Europe in 1874 by an American woman who saw the game played while she was on vacation in Bermuda. She gave tennis its American debut at a club on Staten Island, New York. That same year, the game was also introduced in Massachusetts. Soon tennis was played all over the United States.

Many trends affected the development of sports and recreation during the 19th century. One was the emergence of a solidly entrenched middle class. These people had money and leisure time to devote to sports, either as players or as spectators, and they made possible the emerging sporting-goods industry.

Another factor was philanthropy. The wealthy in America had always been fond of sports, from riding to yacht racing. In the late 1800s enlightened philanthropists tried to make facilities for recreation available to the poor, especially the urban poor, whose children had few places to play besides the streets. Starting in New England in the 1880s, cities began to provide outdoor sand gardens where children could play safely under adult supervision. Boston was the first city to open such a place for children. New York began

Men and women alike enjoyed bowling. This illustration shows an indoor bowling alley around 1870.

advocating the development of playgrounds in 1890, and Chicago's first playground appeared in 1894.

Although playgrounds were at first private ventures, cities soon assumed support of them. Around this time, governments from the federal level down to the localities were coming to recognize that government had an interest in keeping the population healthy, and playgrounds were one way to keep children out of dangerous and unhealthy places.

23

Such harmful places, sad to say, were numerous. Cities of the late 1800s were filthy and often chaotic. Millions of immigrants seeking work in factories were moving into American cities and settling in buildings and neighborhoods where conditions, by modern standards, were scarcely fit for animals. Life there was characterized by drink, disease, disorder, and depression. This situation distressed many Americans, who saw sports—combined with a strong dose of moral instruction—as a possible solution for such urban woes. Reformers saw sports as an antidote to the "immoral" influences youngsters might encounter without the benefit of wholesome outdoor activities.

The health movement also helped to make sports popular. Just as today, America in the late 1800s was enthusiastic about health, and outdoor recreation and exercise occupied the minds and muscles of 19th-century health enthusiasts. Bicycling was seen as especially beneficial. Millionaire John D. Rockefeller, a famous fan of cycling, gave bicycles to his acquaintances as gifts.

This preoccupation with sports and health would bring about great changes in American schools, and thus would reshape education and society for generations to come.

Sports, Schools, and Technology

ALMOST EVERYONE CAN THINK OF A COLLEGE OR university where the athletic department dominates the school. A winning athletic team appears to be the school's main reason for being. Athletes are idolized, and home games are occasions of frenzy.

Even if that description is exaggerated, no one can deny that sports are an important part of school life in America. More than 100 years ago, that was not the case. In the late 18th and early 19th centuries, schools were seen as academic institutions with little or no place for athletics.

That does not mean that students were idle. They were free to pursue recreational activities such as swimming, skating, and various games in what free time they had. It was a long time, however, before schools formally instituted physical education programs and team sports.

Around 1800, a few schools and educators started to look favorably on sports and recreation. Georgetown University reportedly had

The Yale freshman sculling team is seen here at New London, Connecticut, in 1919. American rowing enthusiasts introduced an important innovation—the sliding seat.

fencing instruction as early as 1798, and a facility for a game resembling handball was built there in 1814. Boxing and dancing were also practiced at Georgetown in the early 1800s. Moral considerations, however, placed a limit on the games and sports that students might

Nineteenth-century women athletes could be highly competitive and aggressive at sports.

Early basketball games for women could become a "hullabaloo."

practice. Certain forms of recreation, such as billiards, were seen as corrupting influences.

Gymnasiums and special athletic programs were set up at some schools in the 1820s. Harvard had a gymnastics program, and gymnasium facilities were available at such schools as Brown University and the University of Virginia at about the same time.

In the 1820s boys' schools began programs of exercise and sports. Schools in New England were notable for their early physical education programs. Girls' schools also promoted exercise to some extent in the early 1800s, although games were gentler than at boys' schools. Activities at girls' schools included swimming, badminton, and horseback riding.

Sports and physical education entered the curriculum at women's colleges in the 1860s. Vassar College had a School of Physical Training that included riding facilities, a gymnasium, and even a bowling alley. Activities included gymnastics, archery, and croquet. The rationale behind Vassar's physical education program was that good health was essential to successful academic studies and to developing the mental and moral faculties. Other schools followed Vassar's lead. Soon institutions of higher learning in both the East and the Midwest had programs of exercise and sport for women.

Introducing such programs to women's colleges was not universally approved. Many sports—and, indeed, sport in general—were still seen as masculine domains, and there was opposition to letting women practice them. Some concession to popular feeling seemed advisable. So women's sports were altered slightly so that women would no longer appear to be trying to compete with men on the playing fields.

Among the leaders in bringing sports and exercise to women's colleges was Senda Berenson (1868–1964) of Smith College. Born in Lithuania, she emigrated to the United States and grew up in Boston. She joined Smith College in 1892. Berenson worried that women were deteriorating physically in the new industrial civilization of America. She believed that sports, exercise, and games would help reverse that trend. Berenson also thought that physical exercise would allow

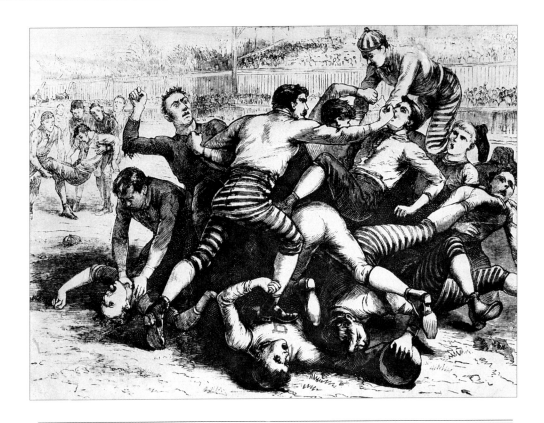

This illustration may be exaggerated, but violence on the playing field was a major concern in the late 1800s.

women to prove that they could perform as well as men, in certain kinds of labor anyway.

Berenson's particular interest was basketball. In 1892 she decided that its rules could be modified for women. Her changes made it a gentler sport and emphasized the importance of courtesy between

Early football games featured no helmets and little padding!

the opposing teams. She also put great emphasis on cooperation within each team and rewrote the rules so that there would be less opportunity for individual players to dominate play. In short, the female players were not supposed to behave like those aggressive,

Yale and Princeton meet at a football match on the New York Polo Grounds in 1881.

glory-seeking men. Berenson went so far as to restrict audiences to women only. She even banned cheers and yells, although she allowed some genteel fight songs.

But efforts to make women's sports gentler than men's were not entirely successful. An aggressive, competitive attitude tended to surface among women as well as men. The first major basketball game at Smith was allegedly a hullabaloo beyond description. The women apparently were not as weak as some people feared.

Basketball quickly became a popular sport for women at the high-school level. It also became the focus, however, of public concerns about competitive sports for women. Those worries had much to do with the winning-is-everything mentality that Senda Berenson decried. In 1901, less than a decade after she brought women's basketball to college, Berenson wrote about the evils of the win-at-all-cost attitude.

In the latter half of the 19th century, men's colleges initiated athletic programs to improve students' health. The programs were successful and grew in both importance and respectability. At Harvard University in 1879, something happened that probably would have been unthinkable a century before: a physical education teacher was admitted to the faculty. Clearly, academic disdain for games and sports was becoming a thing of the past.

Between 1850 and 1870 America saw the beginnings of intercollegiate sports. The first college sports clubs were financed and run largely by students. As noted earlier, rowing was the first intercollegiate sport in the United States, dating from 1852, when Harvard first rowed against Yale on August 3 at Lake Winnipesaukee, New Hampshire. (Harvard won.) On that date, the modern college sports establishment was scarcely even a gleam in anyone's eye.

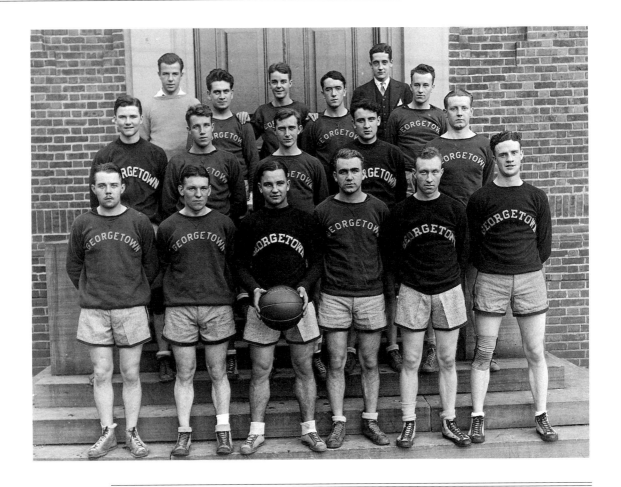

The Georgetown University basketball team in 1927. Early basketball games were played inside a large wire-mesh cage, and this is presumably how basketball players came to be known as "cagers."

According to historians Betty Spears and Richard Swanson, a New York newspaper reporter believed that intercollegiate athletics would never amount to much.

Another famous moment in intercollegiate sports occurred in 1859, at the Amherst-Williams baseball match, one of the earliest sanctioned baseball competitions. The game was played at Pittsfield, Massachusetts; Amherst won. Ten years later, Rutgers and Princeton agreed to meet on the football field. On November 6, 1869, Rutgers won over Princeton in one of the first intercollegiate football competitions. The teams had no helmets and no padding, and there was no crossbar on the goalposts.

From these beginnings, intercollegiate sports grew rapidly. There were problems, however, especially with football. Too many students were injured during games. Also, students who were deeply involved in intercollegiate sports missed classes too often. Early attempts by schools to solve sports-related problems were unsuccessful. In the next decade, however, universities and colleges started bringing their undisciplined athletes under control.

Interscholastic sports for boys became popular in high school in the 1880s and 1890s. The programs were based on student-run associations at first, but the schools soon started hiring physical education instructors who doubled as interscholastic team coaches. Midwestern states were pioneers in high-school sports for boys. Wisconsin is thought to have been the first state to set up a high-school athletic association. By 1900, other midwestern states also had such groups.

Black colleges had their own teams by the late 1800s. One of the first games between two black institutions took place in 1892, when football teams from Livingston College and Biddle University met for

FIRST INTERCOLLEGIATE FOOTBALL GAME

NOVEMBER 6, 1869
WON BY RUTGERS OVER PRINCETON
SIX GOALS TO FOUR GOALS

D.D.WILLIAMSON '70 — E.D.DeLAMATER '71 — S.G.GANO '71 — W.J. HILL '71 — W.S.LASHER '71 — G.E.PACE '71 — C.L.PRUYN '71 — J.H.WYCKOFF '71 — T.W.CLEMENS '72 — E.D.GILLMORE '72 — J.W.HERBERT '72 — G.H.LARGE '72 — W.J.LEGGETT '72 — C.H.STEELE '72

G.H. STEVENS '72 — J.A. VAN NESTE '72 — F.E.ALLEN '73 — M.M.BALL '73 — G.R.DIXON '73 — D.T.HAWXHURST '73 — P.V. HUYSSOON '73 — W.H.McKEE '73 — A.I.MARTINE '73 — C. ROCKEFELLER '73 — J.O.VAN FLEET '73 — G.S.WILLITS '73 — C.S.WRIGHT '70

The first intercollegiate football game, not only in America, but in the world, was played on the afternoon of November 6, 1869 between Rutgers and Princeton at New Brunswick on the Commons between College avenue and Sicard street.

The rules of the game were primitive and the play notably different from that of the developed game. Each team, consisting of twenty five men, was organized with two "captains of the enemy's goal" whose function was to seize all opportunities to kick the ball between the enemy's goal posts, and the remaining players were divided into a squad of "fielders" who were assigned to certain portions of the field, and a squad of "bulldogs" who followed the ball up and down as light infantry where they could do the most good. For Rutgers the "captains of the enemy's goal" were G. R. Dixon and S. G. Gano.

There was no grand stand or bleachers and no admission was charged. Some of the spectators, consisting of undergraduates of the two colleges and their friends, found places on the ground, others at the beginning of the game occupied seats on the top board of a fence which partly surrounded the field. In the course of the play a charge of the light-armed infantry overthrew this fence and brought these spectators also to the ground.

No uniforms were worn save that the Rutgers men had adopted a scarlet turban as their emblem, and one of the Rutgers players, D. D. Williamson, had further adorned himself in a scarlet shirt. For offensive armor they had enthusiasm, and for defensive armor endurance, and 'mid college songs and cheers the Rutgers men won the first intercollegiate football match by a score of six goals to four. The above picture exhibits the portraits of those who took part in this historic game.

A memorial tribute to the first intercollegiate football game, between Rutgers and Princeton, on November 6, 1869. Though the team had no official uniform at this time, the Rutgers men wore scarlet turbans.

a game on Thanksgiving Day. Blacks also played on teams at certain primarily white schools, including Harvard and Oberlin. One prominent black football player of the late 19th century was William Lewis, who played at Amherst and Harvard between 1889 and 1893 and served later as a coach at Harvard.

While sports clubs emerged and the social dimension of sports changed over the years, technology brought about many changes in sports equipment and how the games were played. Vulcanized rubber was developed in the 1830s and improved the performance of rubber balls. Half a century later, in the 1880s, incandescent light made it possible to play sports after dark. New manufacturing technology allowed production of high-quality, standardized sports equipment, while mass production put such equipment within the budget of almost everyone. Transportation technology (specifically, railroads) increased the audience for sporting events by providing access to games in distant cities. Fans in a given town could take the train to a game somewhere else, and professional teams could travel thousands of miles by rail in a single season, playing in numerous cities. Perhaps most important of all, the telegraph made it possible for the press to keep up with sporting events all over the country (and even the world, after submarine cables were put in place across the ocean beds). All these developments helped make America in the late 1800s a nation of sports enthusiasts.

The need for sports equipment brought wealth to Albert Goodwill Spalding (1850–1915), the sporting-goods magnate from Illinois. Spalding and his company did perhaps as much as anyone else to create the American sports culture of our time. A promising baseball player in his teens, Spalding was a professional athlete at 21 and later helped start the National League of Professional Baseball Clubs.

He is best known, however, for the products that bore his name. Spalding went into business in 1876, in partnership with his brother. The business started small but grew quickly through good management.

Spalding also knew how to advertise. It was not enough to say you had a product to sell; Spalding also tied his products to the particular needs of the time. Sports in the 1890s were no longer what they were only a few years earlier. Flimsy, clumsy, homebuilt equipment was no longer adequate. "Do not use homemade equipment when the game calls for something better," Spalding advised consumers.

Here one could see a big change in sports and in society as a whole from the previous century. The Industrial Revolution of the 1800s created factories that could turn out mass-produced consumer goods. It also created a consumer economy where millions of people had enough disposable income to buy those goods and enough leisure time to use them. The growing enthusiasm for sports in 19th-century America created a market for those products. There arose a mass-market sporting-goods industry that would have been all but inconceivable 100 years earlier.

One of Spalding's most clever moves was to publish guidebooks to sports, filled with ads for the company's products. First issued in 1876, the guides were highly successful, and Spalding had to establish whole sports publishing company in 1892. The man hired to run that publishing operation, James E. Sullivan (1860–1914), exercised influence far beyond books and journalism. He also served as an officer of the powerful Amateur Athletic Union, founded in 1888, and became a prominent member of what we would today call the sports establishment. He was a tireless advocate of American athletes in international sports.

A photograph of a scrimmage between Cornell and Rochester universities on October 19, 1889.

By the late 1800s the sports industry and the sports culture of America looked much like what we know today. The mass audience was there. Professional teams had been established. Within this setting, three great games came to dominate sports in America, both in the late 1800s and thereafter: baseball, football, and basketball.

The Big Three: Baseball, Football, Basketball

WHAT WOULD AMERICA BE WITHOUT ITS THREE GREAT professional sports: baseball, football, and basketball? They are wildly popular big businesses in our time, yet they are all 19th-century inventions. Baseball and football developed from earlier games, whereas basketball was largely invented from scratch.

Baseball is one in a long series of games, dating from ancient times, involving attempts to hit a thrown ball with a stick. Such games appear to have originated in the Mediterranean region and spread throughout Spain and France into England. The English at one point played a game called stoolball. It involved a pitcher, called the packer, and a batter, or striker. The pitcher tossed a ball toward an inverted stool. The batter would try to knock the ball aside before it touched the stool. In later versions of the game, the batter had to run to three other stools (the equivalents of modern bases) after he hit the ball.

Stoolball was particularly dangerous. The rules allowed the runner to be called out if a ball was thrown at him and hit him. Despite that risk, stoolball became popular. Its name was later changed to rounders. Apparently, rounders provided the link between modern baseball and the great old British sport of cricket.

This baseball game between the Philadelphia Athletics and the Brooklyn Atlantics on October 22, 1866, ended in a 31-to-12 victory for Philadelphia. Baseball in mid-19th-century America was still far from the huge business it would become in the early 20th century.

By the 1880s, baseball was a major spectator sport. This 1887 illustration shows a game at the New York Polo Grounds.

Similar in many ways to American baseball, cricket involved a batter, pitcher, and catcher, as well as bases (called stakes) to which the batter ran after hitting the ball. Unlike today's baseball bats, which have a round cross section, cricket bats were flat on one side. The British brought cricket to colonial America. After the Revolution, cricket and rounders merged, after a fashion, to become baseball.

By the 1890s, baseball was taking on its familiar modern appearance. Meanwhile, the mass media were devoting more and more attention to sports, and the country in general was going sports crazy.

There were many variations on rounders. One was called town ball. Another was called one old cat. It was also known as two old cat or three old cat, and so forth, depending on how many people played the game and how many bases were involved. As the game's name changed, so did its conventions. For example, cricket stakes were replaced by bags of sand or soil.

Abner Doubleday, war hero and author, is often given credit for inventing baseball, but that story appears to be a myth.

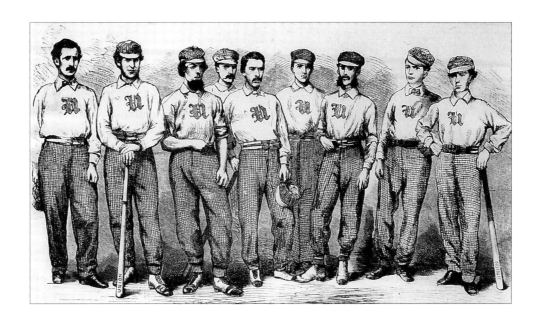

The Union Baseball Club of Morrisania, New York, appears in this 1887 woodcut. The Civil War, which had done much to spread the game around the country, had ended only two years earlier.

Who actually invented the game of baseball? The credit often goes to author Abner Doubleday, but that claim is dubious, as we shall see later. If one person can be called the father of modern baseball, that person is Alexander Joy Cartwright, a 19th-century sports enthusiast who worked in a bank. He helped found the Knickerbocker Base Ball Club, later known as the New York Knickerbockers.

As the club's name indicates, the game was already known as baseball by 1845, when Cartwright drew up rules for playing the game. His rules standardized the sport and the field where it was played. Modern baseball, with its four-base diamond and its nine-player teams, is essentially the same that Cartwright specified. Cartwright's rules were first used in a game at what is now 34th Street and Lexington Avenue in Manhattan. The rest, as the saying goes, is history.

Cartwright and the Knickerbocker club did more than establish a set of rules for baseball. The Knickerbockers also introduced official uniforms—based on cricket outfits—consisting of blue trousers, white shirts, and straw hats. Many other baseball clubs were formed soon after the Knickerbockers. These were made up of amateurs and

Slide! This 1885 illustration shows the winning run in a baseball game. Sports started to become big business about this time.

were essentially social clubs organized around the game. Winning was not everything. The players gathered to have a good time. They behaved like gentlemen and could be fined for arguing over the umpire's decision. Screaming at the umpire, a later tradition, was not allowed. The gentlemanly character of baseball, however, would not last long. A winning mentality soon entered (and, some would say, spoiled) the sport. Many unsavory aspects of baseball, including fights among players and arguments with the umpire, became problems in the 1850s.

The first professional baseball team was the Cincinnati Red Stockings, so-called for the knee-length red stockings the players wore with their white knickers and white shirts. The team was organized in 1866. Three years later, the Cincinnati players received their first paychecks. They played to hundreds of thousands of fans and covered more than 10,000 miles on the road in the 1869 season. In large part, the Red Stockings set the pattern for modern professional baseball, including road trips and big crowds. The big-money aspect of pro baseball, however, was still in the future; in 1869 the team made a profit of less than two dollars.

Like baseball, football on the American model is descended from a European ancestor, namely soccer. The two games are similar and sometimes are even called by the same name, but soccer uses a round ball that may not be touched with the hands, whereas American football uses a ball tapered at both ends for easy grasping and throwing. Although similar games have been played for many centuries, the name "soccer" came into use in the mid–19th century, when a single set of rules for the game was drawn up. How the name originated is uncertain.

48

(continued on page 53)

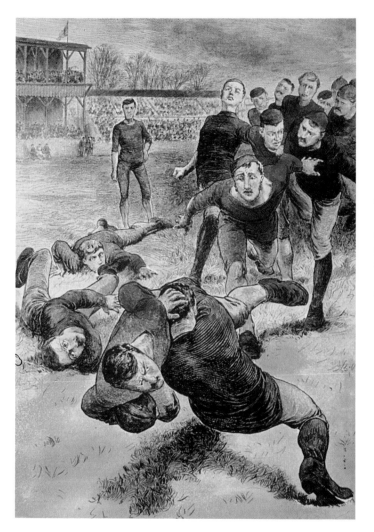

In the 1880s, two American college football teams fight for the ball.

The national pastime is portrayed in this Currier and Ives lithograph.

Baseball being played at the Polo Grounds in New York City in 1887.

A baseball game in the 1880s.

(continued from page 48)

The first college football game in the United States was technically a soccer match. As mentioned earlier, it took place on November 6, 1869, when Rutgers played against Princeton and won, 6–4. Each side is said to have scored a historic first in this game. The Rutgers team wore red caps or jerseys— what might be called the first football uniforms. The Princeton team performed what is thought to have been the first football cheer, adapted from an old army cry used during the Civil War.

Soccer developed into American football through a game called rugby, which allowed players to grasp the ball with their hands. According to one story, the rule against gripping the ball ended one day in 1823 when a student at Rugby School in Warwickshire, England, decided to ignore the rules, grab the ball, and run with it toward the goal. This story may be fiction, but the fact is that a new game called rugby football appeared soon afterward. Under rugby rules, players could run with the ball.

This change surprised Americans at Harvard University when a Canadian rugby team visited there in 1874. American rules prohibited handling the ball, but the Canadians both ran with the ball and used their hands to pass it. This adaptation made the game more interesting. In 1876 the new approach was used in a game between Harvard and Yale. That same year, the newly formed Intercollegiate Football Association adopted rugby rules for the game.

Football became notorious for violence and injuries in the 1890s and early 1900s. Players would confront the opposing team with brutal force. Mass formation plays were especially dangerous. Violence on the field reached a climax in 1905, when 18 players were killed in that single season.

Americans may consider baseball their national pastime, but it owes much to earlier British ball games. This Currier and Ives print shows a baseball game in Hoboken, New Jersey, in 1866.

These accidents, among other problems, led to the formation of the Intercollegiate Athletic Association of the United States (later the National Collegiate Athletic Association). Gradually, rules were changed and safety measures were instituted to make college football less dangerous. As the sport became less hazardous and less controversial, its popularity increased, and college football games became a significant source of revenue for schools. By the end of World War I, college football was played all over the United States.

Whereas football and baseball developed, bit by bit, from earlier games imported from Europe, basketball was different: It was invented in the United States to enhance the sports program of the Young Men's Christian Association. The inventor was Dr. James Naismith, an instructor at the YMCA Training School in Springfield, Massachusetts. In 1891 the school's superintendent, Dr. Arthur Gulick, asked Naismith to invent a new game that would provide a new activity to supplement the YMCA's old regimen of gymnastics. Such activities had little appeal for younger YMCA members, who desired something more exciting. At the same time, Gulick and Naismith wanted to avoid the roughness of sports such as rugby and football. The new game also had to be suitable for indoor play. It had to keep players occupied in the long winter months between the autumn football season and the spring baseball season.

Another kind of ball game seemed like the best idea. But ball games such as football tended to be excessively rough because players were expected to stop—sometimes with bone-jarring force—whoever was carrying the ball. Ideally, the new game would involve a ball but discourage physical contact among players. The answer, Naismith decided, was to throw rather than carry the ball toward a goal. Naismith mounted a peach basket on the balcony of a

By 1902, when this picture was taken, football was beginning to resemble the form it has today, but scrimmages were much more chaotic than today's carefully planned offensive and defensive tactics.

Football outfits, and the ball itself, looked much different in 1880 than they do today.

gymnasium. Then he tossed a soccer ball into the basket from the floor below. That was the first shot in the history of basketball.

In early basketball, the ball remained in the basket after a successful shot, because no one had yet thought to cut a hole in the bottom to let the ball fall through. Someone had to stand on the balcony and reach into the basket to recover the ball. The new game's objective, tossing the ball into the basket, by itself made basketball less violent than other popular ball games. To further reduce the risk of roughness and injury, Naismith wrote rules that kept teams small (only seven players) and included stiff penalties for bodily contact.

Besides the nuisance of retrieving balls from the basket, the new game had other problems. Though Naismith had cut the risk of one player injuring another, there was still a danger of getting hurt by the court itself. Many courts were enclosed by wire mesh, possibly to keep balls from getting stolen when they bounced out among the spectators. In effect, teams played inside a cage. (Evidently this is why basketball players came to be known as "cagers.") Players who ran into the wire could get injured. Some teams wore padded uniforms for protection. Another problem was ineffective backboards. Those were also made of wire mesh. When the ball struck a wire-mesh backboard, it could bounce off in unpredictable

A basketball game at Arkansas State Teachers College. Wooden backboards like the one shown here proved superior to early wire-mesh backboards.

A woman's basketball team, circa 1913, poses for a group photograph.

directions. Eventually wooden backboards took the place of wire mesh, and today Plexiglas backboards are used.

If you could attend a basketball game of the 1890s, you would also notice other differences from today's basketball. For one thing, the pace of the game was slower. Players had to dribble with both hands and they moved about less than in today's game.

As games changed, so did the society in which they were played, and changes in society influenced the games. For example, the central event of 19th-century American history—the Civil War—helped to spread interest in baseball as soldiers played the game in camp. This interest continued after the war and contributed to the rise of professional ball clubs and players.

American society underwent enormous changes in the postwar years. First, there was the transportation revolution as machines replaced horses. Railroads made it easier to travel from the country to the cities. As society became more mobile, manufacturing drew hordes of people into cities to work in factories. Industrial employment required people to live and work by a daily and weekly schedule. That schedule made life more regimented than before. There was a fixed time for work and a fixed time for leisure. To fill their leisure time, millions of people in cities looked toward sports. Moreover, their jobs put money in their pockets, and sporting events were something on which to spend it. Within a few years, a mass audience for professional sports and personal recreational activities emerged.

This huge new audience gave games like baseball the potential to make lots of money for teams and their owners. New technologies for communication, such as the telegraph and telephone, linked cities and helped to expand the nationwide audience for sports. Results of a game in New York could reach Chicago within moments. Mass-market newspapers also did their part to spread sports news everywhere. As a result, in the mid–19th century the amateur sports clubs of earlier days evolved into the mass sports culture of the 20th century, a new form of sports involving big money, big audiences, faster action, and fewer "gentlemen."

The Rise of the Sports Culture

THE MODERN SPORTS CULTURE AS WE KNOW IT STARTED to take shape in the 19th century as professional and collegiate athletics became organized and a media industry arose around them. One can better understand the origins of modern sports culture by looking at the careers of two men: Henry Chadwick (1824–1908) and George Herman Ruth (1895–1948).

Henry Chadwick, one of the fathers of the sports media establishment, was a British immigrant who made baseball popular through his work as a journalist. Some would say that the sports journalist profession started with him. Chadwick moved with his family to the United States when he was in his early teens and spent much of his life in the New York City area. In his youth he became a journalist and chose to promote baseball. He wrote for many newspapers, including the *New York Times*, and for 21 years served as editor of various sports journals.

One of Chadwick's great contributions was to make sports more orderly. He had a vast knowledge of sporting rules and helped to

Indoor lawn tennis at New York's Seventh Regiment Armory in 1881.

formalize the playing of baseball. He also encouraged professionalism and proper moral behavior, and he appears to have viewed the moral aspect of sport as equal in importance to everything else.

In short, Chadwick became known as a champion of the sportsman. The very concept of sportsmanship as something that should bring out a person's nobler traits through athletics may be traced in part to his influence. The sports journalists who came after him were very different from Chadwick, who was described as a dignified, fatherly man who insisted on decency, courtesy, and good order on the playing field. He evidently had little in common with the cigar-chomping reporter who, working in his shirtsleeves with a battered hat tilted back on his head, became the stereotype of sports journalists in later decades. Even in Chadwick's lifetime, sports journalists were becoming a rough lot, in his view. For example, he protested loudly when journalists wrote nasty things about umpires.

Yet sports journalism in America was largely Chadwick's creation. Sports coverage in the mass media still operates by his model, in which the journalist is part of the game, just as the game is part of journalism. As historian Stephen Hardy points out, Chadwick wrote from the viewpoint of an "insider." Chadwick did not merely watch the team and report its activities. He was with the team and involved in its action, even as he described that action for readers.

What a trophy! A giant bat is presented to the Cincinnati Red Stockings, one of the first professional baseball teams.

An engraving of the Chicago Baseball Club made in the 1880s. In the 19th century, informal sporting groups were superseded by professional sports teams.

For Chadwick there was no clear distinction between sports and sports journalism. He was as much a media star as the athletes he covered. If that situation sounds familiar, it should, because that is how sports coverage in our own time operates. The press, radio, and

Sports parks like this one on Staten Island near New York City in 1886 offered spectator sports in a pleasant environment to urban dwellers who wanted to get out of the city. Baseball and lacrosse were among the attractions advertised.

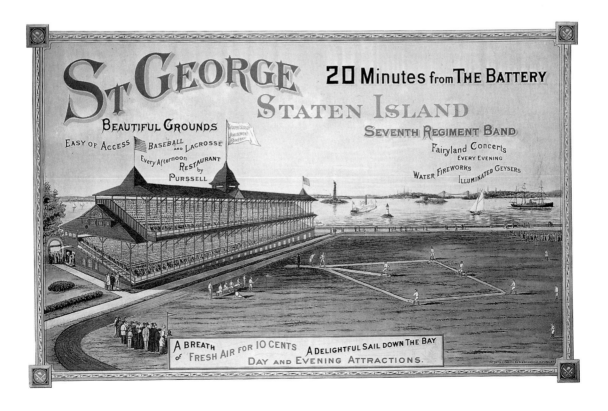

The "Babe"—George Herman Ruth (1895–1948)—was among the first athletes to become a media superstar. The news and entertainment media helped to create his legend, and he in turn helped them by expanding their audience.

television direct their light (so to speak) on every facet of the sports world; and the media, in turn, shine by the reflected light of teams and players. The whole dazzling spectacle has its origins in the work of the 19th-century sports journalist Henry Chadwick.

Tied closely to the rise of sports journalism in the late 19th and early 20th centuries is the emergence of the star athlete. Although early-19th-century athletes such as boxer Tom Molyneux were held in high esteem, certain athletes in the late 1800s and early 1900s drew the attention of the mass media and began to take on what we would call superstar status.

One athlete whose career exemplifies the rise of modern sports culture is George Herman Ruth, better known as "Babe." Thanks to media coverage as well as his own great skills, his name became almost synonymous with baseball, and he himself became the

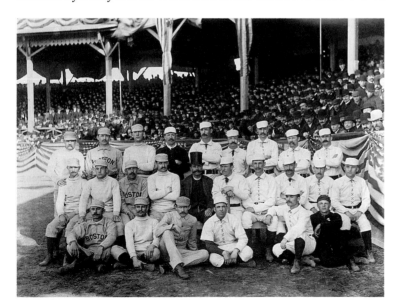

The Boston Red Sox, circa 1886.

quintessential superstar athlete. His legend remains virtually undiminished more than a century after his birth.

Ruth's career in baseball began in 1914 and illustrates how the public's expectations and perceptions of athletes had changed since the late 1800s. Nineteenth-century athletes were supposed to be moral exemplars; at least, that was the ideal. Chadwick, for one, promoted sports as much for moral uplift as for any other reason. Moreover, 19th-century sports players were supposed to look like ideal athletes: lean, lithe, muscular, and dignified, both on the field and off. Old group portraits of teams show players well groomed and well dressed, taking their sport as a serious, highly respectable business. When posing in uniform for pictures, they looked almost like Greek statues of 3,000 years before.

Ruth, on the other hand, was neither a moral paragon nor a figure from classical statuary. Moon-faced and plump, with inelegant manners, he seemed out of place in a business suit. He looked more like a butcher than a star athlete. Tales of his life off the field were less than exemplary, though such stories may have been exaggerated.

Yet the fans identified with Babe Ruth in a way that would have been impossible for an athlete of the Chadwick model. This was partly because, as journalists would say, Ruth made better copy. He was a great athlete but nonetheless had human flaws; and this combination made him perfect for the mass media of the early 20th century. Babe's legend was largely a media creation, while that legend in turn helped to make sports journalism a growing element of the media. He not only helped to create 20th-century sports culture but also embodied a large part of that culture for much of the early 1900s.

68

(continued on page 73)

The 1900 Yale football team.

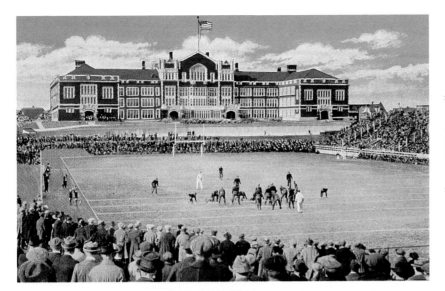

Around 1910, spectators watch a high school football game in Toledo, Ohio.

An early basketball game played in the gymnasium at St. Mary's College in Saint Mary, Kentucky.

At the turn of the century, basketball was promoted as a woman's sport because it was believed to be a less violent and aggressive sport than football.

In the 1890s, schoolboys rough it up in an early game of football.

(*continued from page 68*)

Ruth died in 1948. By that time, in only a century since its beginnings, baseball had gone from the genteel days of the Knickerbocker Base Ball Club to the era of sports superstars. Sport based on the 19th-century model was either dead or dying, and modern sports culture—a product of the sports media establishment—had risen to take its place.

Stephen Hardy, in an essay on sports in American history, sees many different conflicts at work in sports. These conflicts have shaped sports culture. One conflict is that of victory versus "fair play." Playing to win is an understandable goal. A sport without the goal of winning would not be much of a sport. But as 19th-century sports enthusiasts such as Senda Berenson pointed out, it is possible to get carried away and sacrifice everything to a win-the-game mentality.

The attitude that winning is everything is the opposite of what many 19th-century Americans thought sports should be. They viewed sport as a civilized activity where having a good time with friends, rather than winning the game, was the main objective. In modern times, however, that view seems quaint. The sports culture of our day tends to emphasize victory above all else, despite occasional advice to "be a good sport" and take losses gracefully.

Another conflict that Hardy mentions involves the individual versus the team. In team sports, who is more important, the team or the individual player? Most people would say the team, in principle. Yet the sports culture of our time owes its existence partly to superstar athletes who are exalted by the media. Many star athletes are better known than heads of state, and without those stars, their teams might be comparatively obscure and unsuccessful. On the other hand, the star athletes, in most cases, could not play the game alone. They need the cooperation of their teammates, even if the other team members tend to be overshadowed by the stars. When does celebrating individual players become idolatry, and when does it start to weaken the integrity of the team involved? That is something to think about the next time you hear of a player signing a contract for enough money to feed a nation.

Sports Mythology

HISTORY AND MYTH ARE HARD TO SEPARATE AT TIMES. You may be surprised to learn how many stories and beliefs about sports are untrue. Consider the case of Abner Doubleday, who is supposed to have invented baseball in 1839. This tale turns out to be an example of mythmaking in action.

Doubleday is said to have laid out the first baseball diamond in a cow pasture at Cooperstown, New York, when he was a student at a local school. Today the pasture is called Abner Doubleday Field, and the Baseball Museum and Hall of Fame is located in Cooperstown. This is one of the most famous sports stories. It is inconsistent, however, with Doubleday's biography and almost all other evidence about the first baseball game.

In 1839, Doubleday was not a student at Cooperstown. He was a cadet at the U.S. Military Academy at West Point. What is more, baseball appears to have held little or no interest for him. Though he led a full life, becoming an author and a major general in the army, there is no solid evidence that he ever gave much thought to baseball.

As professional sporting organizations arose, outstanding individual players began to develop reputations and acquire groups of admirers.

How did a man with no apparent interest in baseball become known as its inventor?

The transformation of Abner Doubleday from war hero to alleged inventor of the national pastime began around the end of the 19th century, many years after he allegedly turned that pasture into the first ballpark. At this time a public controversy arose concerning the origin of baseball. Patriotic Americans wanted to believe it was a uniquely American game, invented here with no debt to any foreigners. As we have seen, the evidence did not support this view. Baseball developed from earlier games imported from Britain, including rounders.

In saner times the argument probably would have stopped there. The two sides would have agreed to disagree, and that would have been the end of it. But America was going through a phase of intense

Sometimes baseball was actually played indoors. In this illustration, members of Brooklyn's Thirteenth Regiment play baseball in the regiment's armory.

A girl's basketball team from West Virginia, photographed in the early 1900s.

national pride and sought to set itself apart from its European rivals. The result was a cultural war that involved downplaying the influence of Europe on America, even in matters as small as the history of a ball game.

Inflamed by patriotism, the baseball controversy became a focus of intense debate. To settle the matter, a commission was appointed at the suggestion of American sporting-goods manufacturer Albert

This little golf course, built by John Reid in 1888, was the first of its kind in the United States.

Spalding. The commission was assigned to study the origin of baseball and determine how and where the game arose. One member of the commission was Abraham Mills, president of the National League, who was hardly impartial. In 1889 he reportedly claimed, at a meeting in New York City, that baseball was a 100-percent homegrown American sport.

The committee's report, published in 1907, is thought to have been entirely Mills's work. It declared that baseball was indigenous to the United States and was not derived from any foreign games. The

Bowling in a Baltimore alley in 1876. Note the sign that prohibits gambling.

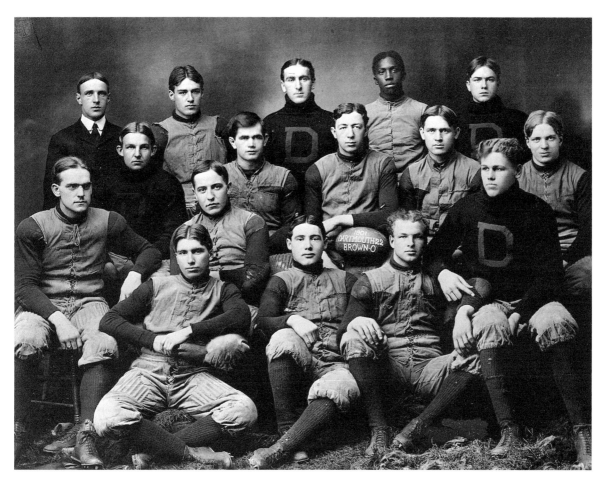

The Dartmouth football team after a 22-to-0 victory over Brown University in 1901.

report also identified Mills's good friend Abner Doubleday as the originator of baseball. Mills described how Doubleday—on a single day in 1839—supposedly turned the clumsy, disorganized ball games of the early 1800s into an elegant sport that became the national pastime.

A whimsical look at gender equality. Two men challenge two ladies to lawn tennis, but the women force the men to accept a handicap.

A determined-looking golfer and her companion in 1903.

What evidence existed for this story? Practically none. Mills based his assertion on a single statement from one Abner Graves, a Cooperstown resident who said Doubleday had invented baseball. But in 1907 Graves was speaking of events almost 70 years earlier. After such a long time, his testimony was dubious at best. Moreover,

83

The Harvard football team of 1890.

Doubleday himself was unable to confirm or refute Mills's story. Doubleday had died in 1898.

Mills's claim, then, was basically unsupported. Yet the story was widely received as fact, and Abner Doubleday became known as the father of baseball. The Baseball Hall of Fame was dedicated at Cooperstown in 1939, 100 years after Doubleday's alleged day of glory in the cow pasture. President Franklin D. Roosevelt even issued a statement honoring Doubleday for originating baseball. Thus a dead general provided the basis for a myth that was based on national pride and an old man's unsupported recollection. America needed a heroic figure to serve as the so-called father of baseball. Abner Doubleday, the war hero, just happened to serve that purpose.

Another and more pervasive myth ties sports to social mobility. According to this myth, success in sports provides an avenue for the poor to rise to lasting wealth, or at least to middle-class status. A child from an impoverished background develops athletic ability and becomes, if not a millionaire, then at least comparatively well-off from his or her prowess at sports.

Such an ascent can happen. After professional sports developed in the 19th century, the possibility of social advancement through athletics gave rise to a popular belief that sports provided a ladder to the top. Ability and hard work supposedly would be rewarded in the arena, where class prejudice was less oppressive than in other professions. It was easier to think that a poor youngster could attain success in sports than to imagine that he would become a bank executive because sports provided a simple meritocracy where success depended more on agility, strength, and perseverance than on wealth, privilege, and social connections.

Over the years, this myth became well established. In their dreams, impoverished city boys could slug their way out of poverty and into prosperity through boxing, or a farm lad from the Midwest could escape the isolation and exhausting labor of rural life by hitting home runs. Yet such success stories were rare. There is little truth to the belief that success at sports will elevate a youth to wealth and fame. Sports historian Steven Riess, in a 1989 essay, explains why.

It is unrealistic, Riess writes, for most young men to think that they can become successful professional athletes. Success in that field is not impossible, but the odds are greatly against it. Openings are few, competition is tremendous, and great effort over a long period is needed. That is why almost all athletes who strive to reach the top will wind up wasting their time and energy. Except for a very few favored individuals, there is no way to get rich playing sports. Even if one reaches the pinnacle of success, the stay there tends to be fleeting—perhaps a couple of years. Then a newcomer arrives, and yesterday's star athlete finds himself forced out of the sports world without any marketable skills to support himself.

To illustrate, Riess examines boxing and prizefighting. Some prizefighters made good money. Jack Johnson received $100,000 for a fight in 1910, and Gene Tunney was paid almost $1 million for a fight against Jack Dempsey. For most fighters, however, the picture was different. Riess cites a study of 127 boxers between 1938 and 1951 that showed that only about 7 percent became nationally known. Another 9 percent attained recognition on the local level, and the vast majority—84 percent—never rose above the bottom rung.

Furthermore, when a boxer did fight for big money, he might actually see none of it. After expenses were met and the fighter's manager was paid, little or nothing of the purse was left. One

A baseball game between the Cincinnati "Red Stockings" and the Brooklyn "Atlantics," in the late 1890s.

lightweight champion in 1948 was paid $65,000 for two fights, but his manager took everything.

To make matters worse, fighters were not known for handling their money wisely. Many of them were inexperienced in matters of personal finance. Some of them spent their winnings quickly on high living and hangers-on. Riess mentions one fighter who won $400,000 during the Great Depression and squandered the whole sum. In another sad story, the great Joe Louis won millions of dollars in the ring but wound up in debt and working at a humble job after his boxing career was over.

Not every successful fighter ended up in quite such lowly circumstances, but the pattern became familiar: a rise to the summit, a moment of glory and wealth, and then a slide back into obscurity and relative poverty. Another survey cited by Riess, involving 15 prominent boxers between 1900 and 1960, showed that about one-third ended up in blue-collar jobs, and the rest had modest white-collar positions. Another study of former champions and contenders who fought in the 1940s produced similar findings. It revealed that one-fourth wound up in blue-collar jobs; about the same percentage owned or worked in bars and taverns; slightly less than one-fifth became managers or trainers; and a few—12 percent—had gone into the entertainment business.

Club fighters without prominent records fared especially poorly. Only about three-quarters of former club fighters in Chicago in the 1960s had steady employment after their boxing careers were over, and most of those men held low-level jobs. In short, Riess points out, the boxing ring is not a route to lasting wealth and fame. It offers only the slimmest chance for brief success, and often leaves ex-fighters physical wrecks and penniless.

To be sure, boxing is an especially bleak and discouraging example. In other sports the prospects are not quite so dismal. At the very least, an impoverished background does not necessarily exclude a would-be pro athlete from the very start, as it would in many other professions. The fact is, however, that sports do not and never did provide much opportunity for rags-to-riches success stories. Such achievement in athletics is about as likely as getting struck by lightning. Advancement is possible, but usually nothing like what the mythmakers say.

All these beliefs are myths. All are untrue. Yet they exert a powerful influence. They are accepted as truth and endlessly fascinate people. The mythology of sports keeps much of the world seated in front of TV screens and in stadiums, watching the play of athletes who are presented almost as divinities.

Sports have come a long way from the gentlemen's clubs and children's town-ball games of 100 years ago. The games of the past were smaller games for a smaller world, where having a good time with friends was more important than winning a match. Today sports are highly commercialized, and a winning record determines which way the money will flow. The sports enthusiast of 100 years ago would hardly recognize not only the way games are played but why they are played. Professionalism has replaced amateurism, and gentility and sportsmanship have declined in importance.

FURTHER READING

Florin, Lambert. *Guide to Western Ghost Towns.* Superior, WI: Superior Publications, 1976.

Hardy, Stephen. "Entrepreneurs, Structures, and the Sportgeist: Old Tensions in a Modern Industry." In *Essays on Sport History and Sport Mythology,* edited by Alan Guttman et al. College Station: Texas A&M University Press, 1990.

Lamar, Howard, ed. *Reader's Encyclopedia of the American West.* New York: Crowell Press, 1978.

Riess, Steven. "Professional Sports as an Avenue of Social Mobility: Some Myths and Realities." In *Essays on Sport History and Sport Mythology,* edited by Alan Guttman et al. College Station: Texas A&M University Press, 1990.

Smith, Don. *How Sports Began.* New York: Franklin Watts, 1977.

Spears, Betty, and Richard Swanson. *History of Sport and Physical Activity in the United States.* Essex, CT: William C. Brown, 1978.

Index

PICTURE CREDITS

DAVID RITCHIE is the author of numerous nonfiction books, including *The Computer Pioneers*, a history of early electronic computers, and the *Encyclopedia of Earthquakes and Volcanoes*. He lives in Baltimore, Maryland.